This Study Belongs TO:

_____

_____

_____

THE
Implanted
WORD

Teresa Ortiz

"Therefore
lay aside
all the filthiness
and overflow of wickedness
and receive with meekness
the Implanted Word,
which is able
to save your souls."
James 1:21

Dear Sisters in Christ,

This study has come together after the Lord prompted me to revisit the book of James and look at it through different lenses than in years past.

I have read through James countless times and studied it in my younger years of faith. It left questions and teachings I was not able or ready to receive at times. Impressions from it in more recent years of study grabbed my heart in greater ways as well as challenged my walk with the Father, or more accurately, He slows His pace to walk with me so I do not fall behind -at least not too far behind.

This time through, however, He opened my understanding in deeper ways, as He has been doing with me in every area of this grand adventure of faith these past two years – and that is to see it through eyes of the eternal and our preparation as His bride and not only "Do" and "Do not", or theology's sake, though they do have their place in the process of transformation into the image of Christ through the renewing of our minds (Sanctification).

Theology and correct understanding are critical in receiving the gospel of Jesus Christ. With that, however, each of us must come to the understanding that we are in need and the eternal life that starts this side of heaven has a grand purpose to transform us into His glorious reflection and goodness for a purified bride and a lost world.

James does not speak to grace as Paul does, but rather assumes as fellow servants and followers of Christ, we understand that our salvation only comes from the grace of God and in that grace, we are , "... His workmanship, created in Christ Jesus for good works, which God prepared beforehand that we should walk in them."

I am praying for all who come across this study at some point. May the good Lord teach us more about His love, character, and eternal purpose. May we receive the implanted word with meekness and understanding. In the mighty name of Jesus, amen.

In Christ,

Teresa

Preface

As we move through the book of James, the goal is to see our eternal purpose and call to be conformed into the image of Christ by living out our faith in practical ways.

James is often misunderstood and has been a source of contention in many areas of the church. It has been said the message of salvation by works is in direct conflict with salvation by grace. Other denominations use James to insist that one is saved by grace and works.

Upon careful study of James, however, many have come to see that his message is in perfect harmony with salvation by grace. His letter is related to faith—that which is received by God's grace so we can believe and respond to His calling on our life. He wrote to believers. Salvation from eternal death was not the concern; they were already born again. It was living the life of a believer – bearing one another's burdens and fulfilling the "Royal Law (James 2:8)" of Christ that he was interested in.

The saving James was speaking of is the daily saving we all need in life this side of heaven. Without action, we cannot be saved from those things that salvation was meant to do. Following through with action is evidence and the ability to receive God's best for us.

James gives practical application and wisdom teaching us how to be "Imitators of God (Ephesians 5:1)". As we will see in week one, James is a direct reflection of Jesus' words in Matthew chapter 5.

It is the exercising of faith that strengthens our life and of those around us. Faith in action grows. Faith without action weakens over time until is it useless –dead, as James said.

In this study we will approach James with the above thoughts and an eternal perspective in mind, having the "Implanted word" as our foundation while we "press toward the goal for the prize of the upward call of God in Christ Jesus (Philippians 3:14)" and live out the royal law of Christ—which is the foundation, I believe, of the message James gave to his brethren…and the church.

Father, open our eyes to see the process in which you worked in

James. May it encourage our own walk and change the way we see, serve, and pray for others; those who know you and perhaps more importantly, those who do not. In the name of Jesus, amen.

STUDY OUTLINE

This study through James is designed for group study and discussion, however, it can easily be used for individual study.

It is structured to study one chapter a week with assignments for 5 days taking between 20-30 minutes each day to complete. The 6th day is a day of reflection and noting questions for discussion with the group and includes a "Deeper Look" section for those who would like to dig a litter deeper and have an opportunity to do so. Day 7 is designed for group discussion.

Though day 7 has preset days/topics to discuss, I encourage each leader to pray and consider the week as a whole and which topics may be best suited for their group as the Holy Spirit leads. Smaller groups may be able to get through all 5 days, depending on needs. The important thing is to stay on topic and glean as much as possible in the time set aside for group study.

My prayer is that this study is friendly and useful for all stages of faith. The format is as follows:

1. Read noted passages.
2. Questions relating to doctrine.
3. Observations – my personal examples / thoughts
4. Questions relating to personal application.
5. Space for personal thoughts, prayer, and confession.

If in-depth study is new for you, do not be discouraged. Pray for the Holy Spirit to reveal His word in new ways. Seek a prayer and accountability partner. It helps. No matter what, do not give up.

There is plenty of room for notes to record insights from group discussion. The Lord will honor every moment we spend time in His word and fellowship with Him and other sisters in Christ.

Table of Contents

"For the word of God is living and powerful, and sharper than any two-edged sword, piercing even to the division of soul and spirit, and of joints and marrow, and is a discerner of the thoughts and intents of the heart. And there is no creature hidden from His sight, but all things are naked and open to the eyes of Him to whom we must give an account."

Hebrews 4:12-13

Preparation

Walking with God has its trials and errors. It is a lifetime of discovery of our Father and who we are in Him and who He is in us. When we try to live out faith in our own strength, we will remain crippled in our view of Christ and the call to walk as He walked and serve as He served—and continues to serve us today.

We cannot live the Christian life on instinct or trusting our heart to lead us to do what is right. God tells us "the heart is deceitful above all things, and desperately wicked; who can know it (Jeremiah 17:9)?" Though we are given a new heart when we are born again, we need to preserve it by tending to it through study, prayer, and actions. For this reason, we must heed the words of Jesus and be diligent to study the scriptures (Matthew 4:4).

For many of us, the Bible is intimidating and, at first glance, impossible to understand. It breeds discouragement, which can lead to defeat before we give it an honest attempt. This is exactly where Satan would have us remain. However, if we remind ourselves that the Bible is a collection of smaller books—many only six to fifteen chapters long—it is not as overwhelming as first supposed.

The Bible is a spiritual book, and most effective when read with a Spirit-filled heart and a desire to allow it to change us, knowing it is filled with everything you and I need to live the life He desires for us. Its very words breathe conviction and joy to our souls.

"For the word of God is living and powerful, and sharper than any two-edged sword, piercing even to the division of soul and spirit, and of joints and marrow, and is a discerner of the thoughts and intents of the heart. And there is no creature hidden from His sight, but all things are naked and open to the eyes of Him to whom we must give an account." Hebrews 4:12-13

"For what man knows the things of a man except the spirit of the man which is in him? Even so no one knows the things of God except the Spirit of God. Now we have received, not the spirit of the world, but the Spirit who is from God, that we might know the things that have been freely given to us by God. These things we also speak, not in words which man's wisdom teaches but which the Holy Spirit teaches, comparing spiritual things with spiritual. But the natural man does not

receive the things of the Spirit of God, for they are foolishness to him, nor can he know them, because they are spiritually discerned. But he who is spiritual judges all things, yet he himself is rightly judged by no one. For 'who has known the mind of the LORD that he may instruct Him?' But we have the mind of Christ." 1 Corinthians 2:11-14

It would be wise to remember the Bible was not written with the intent of a one-time read. God designed it to be studied and meditated upon throughout one's life. What a relief! As the Hebrew passage says, His word is "living and powerful," which means it will be revealed to us on deeper levels as our faith grows.

Preparing my heart for God

Since the word of God can only be understood by having His Spirit moving in our hearts and minds, it is best to prepare them. Following are steps that will help this process. I encourage you to use them each time you approach your study time—not only with this study, but every time you open the Bible.

STEP ONE: Spend some time alone with God. Think about what you hope to gain from this study. In a prayer or a letter, confess all doubt, fear, and any known sin. Tell Him you have (or want to have) a willing heart and are open to all He has for you. If you write a letter, seal it and do not open it until you have completed this study. You will be amazed when you realize how He moved along the way. At this point, if you have not fully surrendered to Christ as your Savior, this is the perfect place to confess your non-belief and ask Him to make Himself known to you during this study (See Psalm 51).

STEP TWO: Ask the Lord to give you a teachable spirit. This is especially important for those who have been a Christian for any length of time. The tendency can be to think, "I've heard this before" or "I already know that." This approach gives the devil a foothold into our life, and we can quickly fall into sin. We should always have the attitude of "what is He going to show me this time?" Ask the Holy Spirit to teach your spirit and give your mind understanding to the truth of His word (Romans 12:1-2).

We have an example of this in Psalm 119:

"Teach me, O' Lord, the way of Your statutes, and I shall keep it to the end. Give me understanding, and I shall keep Your law; Indeed, I shall observe it with my whole heart. Make me walk in the path of Your commandments, for I delight in it." Psalm 119:33-35

Looking at this passage, we can see the two steps mentioned above.

The psalmist made a heartfelt request of the Lord, and his desire was to live as God instructed. We also see his commitment. It is evident that he expected his Lord to respond. It is important to note the psalmist did not say he would follow if it felt right, if it made sense to him, or if it felt good.

STEP THREE: Remind yourself that walking with God is not based on feelings. It is always based on faith and truth. We need to be as the psalmist and say: Lord, show me and I will follow, even if I do not fully understand, even if it does not feel right or make sense to me. Our commitment should be based on God's faithfulness, not our feelings. Remember, as believers we are still able to sin. As a result, His word is always going to challenge us in our sinful behavior. Nevertheless, we can take comfort in the fact that He has given us blessings beyond measure, and we have more peace and comfort from following the way of Jesus than the way of self. Following the example of the psalmist, make your list of requests and your commitment to them.

Requests

1.

2.

3.

Commitments

1.

2.

3.

Father, may we embrace what you have for us and may we choose not to quench the Spirit when He reveals areas of our lives that need transforming. In the name of Jesus, amen.

"Let the word of Christ dwell in you richly in all wisdom and admonishing one another in psalms and hymns and spiritual songs, singing with grace in your hearts to the Lord. And whatever you do in word or deed, do all in the name of the Lord Jesus, giving thanks to God the Father through Him."

Colossians 3:16-17

Week One

The Implanted Word

James and Jesus – Jesus and James

It is widely believed that James, the half-brother of Jesus wrote this letter to the twelve tribes who were scattered abroad at the time of his writing. It would make sense that his heart was toward his brethren – in heritage and in faith.

To understand a greater degree of the passion James displayed, it will help us to spend some time looking to the information provided in the scriptures regarding our brother in time and in Christ.

James and Jesus

Read the following passages, then answer the questions below:

Matthew 12: 46-50
Matthew 13:54-58
John 7:1-5

1) What do you learn about James and his relationship (friend, family, or both) to Jesus?

2) What is his attitude toward Jesus?

3) What does James believe (or not believe) about Jesus?

Read the following passages, then answer the questions below:
1 Corinthians 15:3-7
Acts 15:12-22
Galatians 1:18-19
Galatians 2:6-9

1) What is revealed after Christ's resurrection in 1 Corinthians 15:3-7?

2) What impact do you believe it had on James?

3) In what ways do you see change in James – in attitude and action?

1) What is James' attitude toward Christ?

2) What can you learn from his conversion experience? What does this say to you about the power of seeing Christ, considering His resurrection and its power?

Close out day one in reflection of these passages, write out additional thoughts or Scriptures that come to mind in the context shared as well as a personal prayer:

Day Two

Jesus and James

The book of James is practical in every sense. It is putting our faith to the test and is a call to action as we grow in Christ. James' use of the phrase "Implanted" is interesting as it refers to something that was done by another. We do not implant something in ourselves, we can only do that to/for someone else. Spiritually speaking, James was saying, "receive what God has planted in you". As Paul, said, we were chosen before the foundation of the world (Ephesians 1:4) –First a mocker and non-believer, then a servant of the Lord, as he called himself. This applies to James as well.

God has put eternity in our hearts (Ecclesiastes 3:11), yet only God can initiate and plant in our hearts and minds a desire and ability to know Him.

This thought causes me to consider what kind of planting happened in James while at home with his half-Brother, or while listening to His words when approaching the crowd with other family members. Was he on the sidelines listening to the sermon on the mount (Matthew 5-7)? Was he curious as Jesus taught in the temple? We cannot be certain but it seems plausible. Whether listening firsthand, or being led and taught by the Holy Spirit—or both, it is evident James had a ministry that widely expressed the teachings of Jesus to the Jews.

Before studying the book of James verse by verse, I believe it would serve us well to revisit Matthew chapter 5-7, commonly known as the Sermon on the Mount.

Read Matthew chapters 5-7, then answer the following questions.

1) Based on what you already know about the book of James, what similarities do you see in style and instruction?

2) Do you see these as merely rules to follow or do you see there is a greater purpose?

3) What is Jesus implanting in the hearts and minds of those who were present?

4) Read 1 John 2:1-6 and James 1:25 – What is the result of serving and doing all Jesus commands?

5) How does 1 John 2:1-6 & James 1:25 add to the message of Jesus? What is the purpose of works?

Close out day one in reflection of these passages, write out additional thoughts or Scriptures that come to mind in the context shared as well as a personal prayer:

Day Three

Getting Acquainted

It is important that we approach the book of James with gratitude for what Christ has done for us at the forefront of our minds. Otherwise, it can be discouraging and become little more than a book of rules instead of a message based on God's love. Remembering the overall purpose for good works, which is the perfecting of our faith and being prepared as a pure bride, will help us to understand the entire context of the message James gave to his brethren—the Jewish believers—and to us if we have had our "me and Jesus, Jesus and me" moment. For there is no distinction between Jew and Gentile in Christ Jesus (Ephesians 2).

Today's assignment is to read the entire book of James – take it at face value. For this readthrough resist the temptation to stop and study, take notes, read commentaries, or hold closely what you already know about the book.

May the Lord give us eyes to see and ears to hear as if this were our first time reading this letter.

Close out day one in reflection of these passages, write out additional thoughts or Scriptures that come to mind in the context shared as well as a personal prayer:

Day Four

Mind set

"I beseech you therefore, brethren, by the mercies of God, that you present your bodies a living sacrifice, holy, acceptable to God, which is your reasonable service. And do not be conformed to this world, but be transformed by the renewing of your mind, that you may prove what is that good and acceptable and perfect will of God." Romans 12:1-2

Think back on yesterday's read through of the book of James and your closing prayer.

1) What thoughts and feelings come to mind at this moment?

2) Think about your requests and commitments from the preparation section at the beginning of this study. Has anything changed in consideration of what we have covered up to this point?

3) How will you approach James this time that will be different from previous studies? Write out the differences. If this is your first study of James, write out your purpose in doing this study.

Close out day four in prayer and setting your mind on Christ, allowing the Holy Spirit to prepare you for what He has for you in studying James. Confess any doubts, fears, and challenges you have had in your walk that you would like to be strengthened, healed and free of in this season of your life.

Day Five

Repeat – Receive – Record

Read the entire book of James. During this read through, stop each time you come to something that provokes emotion. Put a question mark by the verse (or in a notebook), then record them based on the steps below.

Answer the following questions as you record these verses.

1) What emotion is provoked?
2) Why do you think this is?
3) What part of it is challenging?

These questions will help define areas of our soul that are still wounded. The purpose of this assignment is to help us be aware of blind spots in our faith so we can seek the Lord for complete healing and restoration, and to help us live the life of love God calls us to while moving toward victory over those wounds.

Use the space below to record your findings as you read through James – the back side of this page is blank for this same purpose:

Read – Receive – Record – Continued:

Close out day five with prayer. Record any additional thoughts, again committing your mind and heart to receive as we move into our closer look at the book of James.

Day Six

Reflect on this week's assignments. Make note of questions or thoughts you would like to share during group discussion. If you are doing this study on your own, write out a prayer of things you would like clarity on and ask the Holy Spirit to reveal the word through continued study, your pastor, or through a faithful friend or family member in Christ.

1)

2)

3)

4)

"Let the word of Christ dwell in you richly in all wisdom and admonishing one another in psalms and hymns and spiritual songs, singing with grace in your hearts to the Lord. And whatever you do in word or deed, do all in the name of the Lord Jesus, giving thanks to God the Father through Him." Colossians 3:16-17

Day six challenge: Read the book of James again.

Day Seven

Discuss this week's assignments and hold each other accountable in grace and prayer during this study (and always).

Discussion notes:

"Do not be deceived, my beloved brethren. Every good and perfect gift is from above, and comes down from the Father of lights with whom there is no variation or shadow of turning."

James 1:16-17

Week Two
The Implanted
Work

The Implanted Work-James Chapter 1

Now that we have read the book of James at least two times, if not three, we will slow our pace and focus on one chapter per week. First, reading the entire chapter and then breaking it down even further by subject sections (verses). Pray before you begin. Be prepared to set aside 30-45 minutes if possible, for day one.

Day One

Chapter Highlights and Theme/s

Read James chapter one, then answer the following questions

1) Who is the author and how does he identify himself?

2) To whom was the letter addressed? What does this reveal about his heart?

3) What subjects/concerns does he address? (Watch for repeated phrases)

4) Which Persons of the Godhead did James mention? What do we learn about their character and role?

a)	b)
1.	1.
2.	2.
3.	
4.	
5.	
6.	
7.	
8.	
9.	
10.	
11.	
12.	
13.	
14.	
15.	

5) What law is mentioned in this chapter and how is it described?

6) What actions are mentioned – Positive and negative and what are the results of each?

Positive/Result	Negative/Result
1.	1.
2.	2.
3.	3.
4.	4.
5.	5.
6.	6.
7.	7.

Close out day one in reflection of what you have read and your initial thoughts. Write out a prayer – in humility and honesty, share your thoughts with the Lord.

Day Two

"But let patience have its perfect work, that you may be perfect, lacking nothing." James 1:4 – This, dear sister, is the purpose of the implanted work.

Keeping the highlights of the entire chapter in mind, our next step is to break it down even further, remembering to avoid commentaries and use cross references instead. They will be listed in parenthesis next to the question as well as within the body of others.

Read verses 1 -11, then answer the following questions. (Cross references)

1) What are the three directives found in vs 2, vs 4, vs 5, and vs 6 given by James?

a.

b.

c.

2) How should we do (work) them? What result can we expect, both positively and negatively based on our actions? (Vs 6-7)

"My brethren, count it all joy when you fall into divers temptations, knowing this, that the trying of your faith worketh patience." James 1:2-3 KJV

The King James Version uses two different words – words I believe add great value to James' opening statement. He gets right to the point and the heart of the matter.

"Count" is a mathematical term, meaning to evaluate – how much do I have in front of me? What can I do with it? If used wisely, how will it add value to me? It is also a reckoning (coming to terms with what has happened) In the spiritual sense, this does not imply loss, or little, but great value – God's absolute best, holding nothing back.

"Temptation" is a stronger word for trial – it is the challenge (trial) that comes our way in which we have a choice in how to respond. Will we be double-minded (saying we trust God, but doing our own thing instead) or will we be single-minded and stable, no matter what comes our way?

"…And lead us not into temptation, but deliver us from evil…" Matthew 6:13

Read 1:2-8 again with these thoughts in mind, then answer the following questions.

1) What is the value of trials? (1 Peter 1:3-7; Romans 5:1-5)

2) Explain the promise (Vs 5) we receive when asking in complete faith? (Proverbs 2, 3:3-8, 13-18) How is it given and by whom?

3) What does it mean to be double-minded? Why does doubting cause instability? Give a personal example. (Matthew 6:24; Matthew 23:25-28; 1 Corinthians 10:21)

4) Based on your understanding, write out James 1:2-8 in your own words. What is the Holy Spirit speaking to you (Keep it in context of James' message)?

5) Read verses 9-11. How do these verses relate to 1-8? What point do you see James was making? (John 16:33, Acts 17:24-31; Hebrews 9:27)

Close out day two with reflection and prayer. Record your thoughts and any additional scriptures that come to mind:

Day Three

"...Being confident of this very thing, that He who began a good work in you will complete it until the day of Jesus Christ." Philippians 1:6

"And I heard, as it were, the voice of a great multitude, as the sound of many waters and as the sound of mighty thunderings saying, 'Alleluia! For the Lord God Omnipotent reigns! Let us be glad and rejoice and give Him glory, for the marriage supper of the Lamb has come, and His wife has made herself ready'. And to her it was granted to be arrayed in fine linen, clean and bright, for the fine linen is the righteous acts of the saints. Then he said to me, 'Write: Blessed are those who are called to the marriage supper of the Lamb!' And he said to me, 'These are the true sayings of God' Revelation 19:6-9

Endurance is a choice – a choice easily made when we understand God's loving purpose for the work He is doing in His children. Keep in mind; the message of James is not how to become a child of God (Being born again—saved) His concern is our response to love (salvation) and the sanctification process.

Read James 1:12-18, then answer the following questions.

1) What is the blessing and promise of God? How is it received?

2) Read 2 Timothy 4:8; 1 Corinthians 9:25; James 1:12; 1 Peter 5:2-4; 1 Thessalonians 2:19. List all crowns mentioned. (Challenge: read several verses before and after the noted passages). What do they have in common?

a.

b.

c.

d.

e.

3) In theses verses we see a contrast of God's character and gifts He gives. Make a list of both:

GOD DOES NOT DO/GIVE	GOD DOES DO/GIVE

4) Who is responsible for our actions? What is the progression? List it in order.

5) Read verse 2 and 12 again. Do you see a greater correlation between temptation and trials? Give a personal example.

6) How does being double-minded fit into our ability to endure? Is it related to verses 13-15?

7) Read verses 1-18 again. What are some of the good and perfect gifts listed in this passage? You may have already listed some in question three, still list them again until they are sealed on your heart and mind.

8) Read the following passages and note how they add to verses 16-18

a. 1 Corinthians 10:12-13:

b. Ephesians 1:3-6:

c. 2 Peter 1:2-4:

d. Psalm 18:28-35:

9) How do these passages encourage / challenge you to be single-minded (faithful; not wavering)?

God's word applies to every area of our life.

*What are you facing this season?

*How can what you just studied give you comfort and confidence?

We live in a fallen world. Whether by our own actions or those of others, God will use what we face to purify us if we are willing to let patience have its perfect work in us.

Close out day three with reflection. Share your thoughts with the Lord.

Day Four

"But he who looks into the perfect law of liberty and continues in it, and is not a forgetful hearer but doer of the work, this one will be blessed in what he does." James 1:25

The work we do IS living out the law of liberty – which is the love and grace of God, which brings freedom as we will see in today's assignment.

Read James 1:19-25, then answer the following questions.

1) We are given specific instructions in verse 19 that should be a response to what we learned in verses 1-18. Read the cross-referenced passages for each directive in verse 19. How do they add clarity to verse 19? To whom is this referring in terms of our response? Write out your thoughts.

a. Swift to hear (Isaiah 30:21; Habakkuk 2:1; 1 Kings 19:11-13; 2 Timothy 2:3:16; Revelation 3:20)

b. Slow to speak (Proverbs 16:21; Proverbs 17:28; Job 30-31; 38-40:5)

c. Slow to anger (Psalm 37:8; Proverbs 14:29; Proverbs 15:1; Proverbs15:18; Proverbs 29:22

"This you know, my brethren. But everyone must be quick to hear, slow to listen and slow to anger;" James 1:19 NASB

"This you know" as rendered in the NASB (New American Standard Bible) or "So then" in the NKJV (New King James Version), in context is referring to all James just spoke about endurance and blessing through being perfected in our temptations and trials. God gives us good and perfect gifts; He holds nothing back…. Standing firm in this truth should cause us to slow down and listen to the Lord and not be too quick to question Him in anger or lack of understanding, which can result in anger toward Him. This leads to doublemindedness, leading to sin, and ultimately the righteousness of God in us is silenced as verse 20 tells us. The truth is, unless we first seek to understand the perfect will of God for us (being transformed into His image), and His royal law of love, we will not be able to practice our faith and apply verse 19 to others. First and foremost, it must penetrate our hearts and minds, otherwise, our works will be strained and become an imperfect law of obedience (obligation) instead of the perfect law of liberty (freedom and gratitude).

James 1:1-20 speak to our internal response: mindset and unwavering faith, while James 1:21 through chapter five speak to our outward response: mindset and faith in action. Remember, the salvation spoken of throughout refers to everyday life. The saving (sparing, deliverance and delivering ourselves and others from pain), of our souls, not our spirit. Being born-again, will be evidenced (proven, or justified, as James put it) by our actions.

1) Who and what is the "implanted word"? (John 1:1; Deuteronomy 8:1-3; Jeremiah 31:33; Ephesians 5:1-2)

2) How does receiving the implanted word and living out this word save our soul? (1 Peter 2:11-12; 1 Peter1:22-23; 2 Peter 2:7-8)

3) Read James 1:4-6. Then read James 1:22-24 again. What are some of the reasons we would not receive (remain in) the implanted word? How do verses 4-6 add understanding to the idea of forgetting who we really are in Christ?

4) What is the "perfect law of liberty?" And what is the "work" being referred to in James 1:25? (John 6:28-29; Romans 8:2; 2 Corinthians 3:4-6, 16-17; Galatians 5:13; 1 Peter 2:15-17)

Jesus, being perfect is our liberator. He freed us from the law of sin and death. He gave us a new spirit and brought us out of darkness into light, and out of bondage into freedom and is God's representation of love. Remaining in this truth should cause our hearts to pass it on through our actions toward others as a reflection of what Christ did for us.

What are your closing thoughts? Record them here and end this day in prayer:

Day Five

James was speaking to Jewish believers. They were familiar with the law. Perhaps many of them sat under the Pharisees and saw examples of pride and arrogance disguised as religion. Do and Do Not. It was common in the days of Christ that many focused on outward actions instead of the inward attitude of the heart. Jesus made this clear when He rebuked the leaders, calling them white-washed tombs.

It is interesting that James followed his message on receiving the implanted word with meekness with useless and true religion. What is the message to you and me?

Read verses 26-27, then answer the following questions.

1) To what is James referring in verse 26? Give an example or two.

2) What are the three things which qualify as pure and undefiled religion?

3) Which come easy to you? Which are difficult? Why is this?

Unspotted from the World

I believe James closed out his thoughts on the purpose of trials by finalizing the three-fold response every believer should have in living as a doer of the work of faith:

a. Ask for wisdom to persevere and make the right choices
b. Receive the implanted word with meekness
c. Live out love – outwardly and inwardly. (Single-mindedness & integrity)

Read James chapter 1 again, then answer the following questions.

1) List the tools provided throughout this chapter that will help keep ourselves unspotted (not accepting or participating) from the world.

2) Read the following passages, how do they provide additional tools or further explain what it means to keep ourselves "unspotted" from the world and add strength to all of chapter 1?

a. Romans 12:2:

b. Galatians 5:16-26:

c. 1 Peter 1:13-21:

Day Six

Wisdom and the Father of Lights

"Do not be deceived, my beloved brethren. Every good and perfect gift is from above, and comes down from the Father of lights with whom there is no variation or shadow of turning." James 1:16-17

In one of our assignments this week we touched on the good gifts God gives us—one being wisdom. We did not dive into the topic of how God gave wisdom to the priests in the Old Testament, nor did we reflect on the phrase, "Father of lights." If you have the time, I encourage you to read the following passages as I believe they add renewing strength to our understanding of our heavenly Father's character. When we know the One in whom we believe, we will grow in confidence and stability, which will lead to victory and healing for our souls. Our faith will increase and 'counting it all joy" will become easier as we live out the implanted work of God.

Wisdom in the Old Testament – The Urim and the Thummin

Urim = Lights
Thummin = Perfect Knowledge

(James 1:5)

1. Exodus 28:29-30
2. Leviticus 8:8-9
3. Deuteronomy 33:8
4. 1 Samuel 28:6 (Saul asked for the wrong reasons – he doubted God's plan)
5. Ezra 2:63
6. Nehemiah 7:65

The priests in the Old Testament were instructed to design and wear specific garments when ministering to the Israelites. One being the Breastplate of Judgement, which had twelve stones on the front representing each tribe.

The Urim and the Thummin, two additional stones, were placed on the breastplate as well. These represented the Father of Lights – the One with perfect knowledge. As the priests inquired of the Lord, it is believed these two pieces would light up in answer to the inquiry. Exactly how it worked is unclear, but we see from the passages noted, it was given by God and used by the priests.

God's provision for wisdom is further completed under the New Covenant, through the indwelling of the Holy Spirit, who is our breastplate of judgement (John 15:26-16:15) as Jesus explained. The Holy Spirit is one of the many gifts from the Father of lights. Father of Lights

1. John 1:4, 9
2. John 8:12
3. 2 Corinthians 4:4-6
4. 1 Peter 2:9
5. 1 John 2:8
6. Ephesians 5:8-9
7. Romans 13:12

1) What do these passages speak to you? How do they bring you renewed hope, strength, and courage?

In Christ, we are the children of Light. When I consider James chapter one, I am comforted in knowing God desires me to be perfect and complete so that I lack nothing because He loves me. He is the Father, and I am one of his many lights. What a beautiful reminder. I pray this is a great reminder to you as well. May we be encouraged to live our faith out of gratitude for what He has already done, not out of fear that we may not be saved if we do not do enough. Praise His name.

Day Seven

Discuss this week's assignments and hold each other accountable in grace and prayer during this study (and always).

Discussion notes:

"You see then that faith was working with his works, and as a result of the works, faith was perfected."

James 2:22

Week Three
The Implanted Law

Day One
Getting Acquainted

Read James chapter two, then answer the following questions.

1) What themes/subjects did James mention?

2) Which laws did James mention? How do they differ? How are they the same?

3) In context of "work" related to the law of liberty, how do you see James' use of the word "Justified": As in declared righteous before God (Born-again) or Evidence (Proof of salvation and faith)? Explain your answer.

4) What do you learn about the Father? Note all His attributes, gifts, and callings you can find.

5) Read chapters 1 and 2. How does chapter one give context and understanding to the topics in chapter two?

Close out day one in reflection and prayer – record your thoughts:

Day Two

Personal Favoritism and Motives

1) What causes us to become judges with evil motives? Write out the details James mentioned? What are some of the evil motives?

2) How does what we see and do contrast with what God sees and does? (1 Samuel 16:7; James 4:6-8)

3) Why do you suppose God chooses the poor of this world? In what ways can we be poor? (Matthew 5:3; 1 Corinthians 1:26-31)

James was speaking of the outwardly appearance that reveals a person is poor, but he took it to a deeper meaning when he spoke of why God chooses the poor:

POOR = lacking money; humble state; inadequate in character; recognizing our need.

4) How does considering the deeper meaning of poor add understanding to verse 4? How does it relate to dishonoring a poor man?

5) What is the general nature of a rich man? (Mark 10:17-27)

6) What is the attitude in which we should hold our faith? In what ways are you challenged by vs 1-7?

7) Using your concordance, look up passages that speak to this same subject. Note the passage and how it adds to the heart of this message.

Close out day one in reflection and prayer – record your thoughts:

Day Three

The Three Laws

Read James 2:8-13, then answer the following questions.

1) What three laws are mentioned? How are they described?

a.

b.

c.

2) Read the following passages and note how they add to the three laws mentioned and which fit under which law best.

a. Matthew 7:12:

b. Leviticus 19:18:

c. Exodus 20:1-17:

d. Galatians 5:6 and 6:2:

3) Read James chapter 1 – 2:13. Take special note of the verses that begin with the words, "So", "But", "If", and "Let". Record the verses that have a positive result. What do they have in common?

4) What law is referenced in chapter one and chapter two. What is the message James was sending up to this point in the letter?

5) Read James 2:13; Proverbs 21:13; Matthew 5:7. What is the message here? What is lacking in our lives if we do not exercise mercy the way God has shown us mercy?

Close out day one in reflection and prayer – record your thoughts:

Day Four

1) How does this section challenge your understanding of salvation by grace? To what kind of saving do you believe James is referring? (Keep the previous verses in mind.)

Write out your thoughts:

2) Consider these two phrases: "What use is it" and "Being by itself" (1 Timothy 4:6-11; Hebrews 5:12-6:2) Faith is present, that is not the issue. What hinders and causes that faith to die—become useless?

It is important for us to remember that James was speaking to believers who understood they have been born-again by the grace of God. Their spirit was saved, but they had not yet experienced the outcome of their salvation—just like us today. On this side of heaven, it is a process. Only from God's perspective is it complete. Our soul is healed in the perfecting of our faith – Our faith does not grow if we do not exercise it as we just read, so what is the conclusion?

3) Read James 1:21, James 2:13, and 1 Peter 1:9. How does 1 Peter 1:9 fit in? How do these verses add understanding to the phrase "Can his faith save him?" Read vs 8-17.

Close out day four with reflection and prayer. Record your thoughts:

Day Five

Faith That Works is a Faith That Grows

"You see then that faith was working with his works, and as a result of the works, faith was perfected." James 2:22

Read James 2:18-26, then answer the following questions.

1) How can faith by itself be seen? Is evidence required? Explain your answer.

2) In giving examples, what point was James making?

3. Explain your understanding of verse 24.

4) How does James wrap up chapter 2? What was his main admonishment (gentle correction) to the believers? Why do we need it today?

Justify/Justification

These words have two different meanings. One relates to theology and the salvation by grace alone, and the other relates to evidence that proves innocent or guilty, or a belief system.

Salvation by grace alone through Justification: Christ proclaimed us right before God. It is God's doing, and His alone and is made available to all who believe.

Justify: To make a point by way of action. It is the evidence (assurance) that accompanies a particular claim. It can give a good or bad name to a person.

5) Read the passages below. Note how they add understanding to verses 20-24.

a. Hebrews 11:1-2:

b. Hebrews 12:1-2:

c. Romans 4:1-25:

d. Galatians 2:16-21

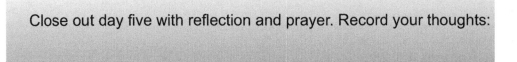

Close out day five with reflection and prayer. Record your thoughts:

Our faith is evidenced and perfected by the work we do. Not out of obligation or to gain favor with God, but out of the gratitude of our hearts in response to the Word who has been implanted in our hearts—Jesus Christ, by the Holy Spirit. When we remember this and walk in it, we will be fulfilling the royal law. If, however, we never grow and our desires never change, then we must consider – are we truly dead and without the Spirit of God, as James compared in verse 26? May the evidence of our salvation be experienced by others and may our souls continually be saved and healed until the Day of redemption. In the name of Jesus, amen.

Day Six

The Lord of Glory and that Noble Name

James began chapter two with a powerful statement and though His message was focused on practical faith and not the Deity of Christ, his statement implied His Deity should be the core of putting faith into action. For this reason, I believe it would do us good to remind ourselves of whom it is we believe – as Paul said, *"I know in whom I believe (2 Timothy 1:12-14).* He followed an admonishment with a statement about "that noble name by which you have been called", vs 7. It is also worth exploring a little bit more, in my opinion.

The Lord of Glory

Read the following passages. How do they add to verse 1 and more importantly, how do they challenge and encourage you to live out your faith in grace and love toward others?

1. Psalm 24:1-10
2. Psalm 29:1-11
3. Isaiah 44:6-8
4. 1 Timothy 6:10-15

That Noble Name

Read the following passages. What do they have to say about "that name"? Note how they challenge and encourage you to answer this call to action.

1. Acts 11:15-26 (Peter speaking)

2. 1 Peter 4:14-16

This is receiving the implanted law.

May we serve others with gladness, for when we do, we are serving the Lord by "letting our light so shine among men so that when they see our good works, they will glorify our Father in heaven." Matthew 5:15-16

Day Seven

Discuss this week's assignments and hold each other accountable in grace and prayer during this study (and always).

Discussion notes:

"Who among you is wise and intelligent? Let him by his good conduct show his [good] deeds with the gentleness and humility of true wisdom." James 3:13 Amplified Bible

Week Four
The Implanted Wisdom

Day One

Getting Acquainted

Read James chapter three then answer the following questions.

1) What three topics did James address in this chapter?

2) What attributes/characteristics about God did James mention?

3) What contrasts did James make?

4) How does the last verse in this chapter compare to the last verse

in chapter two? What is another word for "fruit"?

5) Read James chapter 1-3. What is the foundational theme? Write out one or two verses that you see connect each chapter with the foundational theme in mind.

6) What are the repeated words or phrases in the chapter? Compare the instruction given in James chapter 1:5 with this chapter. What is the message?

7) Considering wisdom and verse 13, why do you believe teachers will receive stricter judgment? What does verse 1-2 have to do with the rest of the chapter?

Close day one in reflection and prayer. Write out your thoughts:

Day Two

The Tongue – a fiery dart

1) What do bits, rudders, and tongues have in common? Do they function on their own?

2) Explain your understanding of verse six.

3) Why do you suppose man can tame animals, but not his own tongue?

4) Consider who holds the reigns on a bit or a steering wheel that directs the rudder. What is the implication regarding "no man can tame his own tongue"?

5) Read vs 5-6, Matthew 15:15-20; Ephesians 4:17-32; 1 Peter 2:1; Ephesians 6:10-18. To whom must we relinquish control of our tongue? By whose power is it tamed?

James was addressing his brothers and sisters in Christ who had become discouraged because their hardships were tempting them to turn away. It would appear from this section they began to hurt one other with their words and actions, reverting to their old ways. Things are the same today. We see Christians treating one another terribly with assaults of the tongue. I believe James was reminding them how wicked within ourselves we can be. How can we rule over our tongues?

6) Read James 1:21-26 and James 2:8. How does this encourage us to remember who we are?

Close out day two with reflection and prayer. Write out your thoughts:

Day Three

Blessing and Cursing – the tongue continued

1) What examples of contrasts does James give in verses 9-12?

2) How do these contrasts explain a believer versus a non-believer? (Galatians 5:13-24)

3) In what ways do we bless and curse? (James 3:6; Proverbs 11:9, 11,17, Proverbs 15:1-2, and Proverbs 18:4)

4) What is the point in these examples?

Close out day three in reflection and prayer. Write out your thoughts:

"The law of the LORD is perfect, restoring the soul; The testimony of the LORD is sure, making wise the simple. The precepts of the LORD are right, rejoicing the heart; The commandment of the LORD is pure, enlightening the eyes. The fear of the LORD is clean, enduring forever; The judgments of the LORD are true; they are righteous altogether. They are more desirable than gold, yes, than much fine gold; Sweeter also than honey and the drippings of the honeycomb. Moreover, by them Your servant is warned; In keeping them there is great reward. Who can discern his errors? Acquit me of hidden faults. Also keep back Your servant from presumptuous sins; Let them not rule over me; Then I will be blameless, and I shall be acquitted of great transgression. Let the words of my mouth and the meditation of my heart be acceptable in Your sight, O LORD, my rock and my Redeemer."

Psalm 19:7-14

Day Four

Wisdom and Knowledge

1) Looking back at verses 8-12, what do you believe is the reason behind James' question? Could it be rhetorical?

2) What kind of wisdom is James describing? List each attribute mentioned.

3) What kind of person is James describing? In what/who is this person walking? Read the following passages and note how they add understanding to James 3:14-16.

a. Isaiah 5:18-24:

b. Romans 8:1-2:

c. Ephesians 2:1-3:

5) Read James 3:8-4:10. What continual battle does it appear James is describing? (Matthew 26:41; Galatians 5:17)

6) Read vs 13 again. What is the contrast in this verse and 14-16?

Close out day four in reflection. How does this challenge you regarding our season as a country and the current state of the body of Christ? Write out your thoughts and prayer.

Day Five

Wisdom from Above

Who among you is wise and intelligent? Let him by his good conduct show his [good] deeds with the gentleness and humility of true wisdom." James 3:13 AMP (Amplified Bible)

Read James 3:17-18, then answer the following questions.

1) To what kind of wisdom is verse 17 referring? List all its attributes.

2) How does vs 13 tie into verses 17-18? How are we to show our deeds—live out our faith? (Matthew 11:29-30)

3) Look up the following words. How do they reveal the character of Christ?

a. Meekness:

b. Gentleness:

c. Humility:

4) To whom is the 'seed' referring? (Matthew 5:9) Read the following verses. Note how they add value or understanding to verses 17-18.

a. Psalm 22:26:

b. Psalm 25:9

c. Psalm 147:6

d. Psalm 149:4

e. Romans 14:13-21:

b. Philippians 2:3-8:

Close out day five with reflection and prayer. Write out your thoughts:

Day Six
Deeper Look

"Does a fountain send out from the same opening both fresh and bitter water? Can a fig tree, my brethren produce olives, or a vine produce figs? Nor can salt water produce fresh." James 3:11-12

The Fountain of Life – Fresh Waters

The book of James is believed to be one of the earliest letters to the church. It is rich in Old Testament thoughts and proverbs as well as filled with the words of Jesus amplified. It makes sense, then because Jesus used water and fruit trees as examples when pointing out differences between good and evil; love and hate; light and darkness, that James did as well. In essence he was telling his brothers and sisters in Christ that their actions were sending mixed messages and they were not being a "fountain of living water" when acting double minded.

Again, James echoed Jesus in John 4:10:

What do the scriptures have to say about fountains (springs) and fruit? Read the following passages. Note who they add value to James 3:11-12. How do they highlight the royal law?

1. Zechariah 13:1
2. Proverbs 10:11
3. Proverbs 25:26
4. Jeremiah 2:13
5. Psalm 36:9
6. Deuteronomy 8:7-8
7. John 15:15
8. John 7:38-39
9. Titus 3:3-9

"And it shall come to pass in that day, that the mountains shall drop down new wine, and the hills shall flow with milk, and with waters, and a fountain shall come forth of the house of the LORD, and shall water the valley of Shittim." Joel 3:18

Write out your thoughts:

Day Seven

Discuss this week's assignments and hold each other accountable in grace and prayer during this study (and always).

Discussion notes:

"Or do you think that the Scripture says in vain, the Spirit who dwells in us yearns jealously"? But He give more grace. Therefore He says: 'God resists the proud, but gives grace to the humble."

James 4:5-6.

Week Five
The Implanted
Spirit

Day One

Echoes of the Sermon on the Mount
Jesus and James Revisited

Read James chapter four, then answer the following questions.

1) What themes/topics did James mention in this chapter?

2) What contrasts are made? List them.

3) What promises are made; how are they obtained?

4) Read Matthew chapters 5-7. With the sermon on the mount (Matt. 5-7) and James chapter four in mind, note at least four verse/passages from Matt 5-7 that connect the attitude of the heart and mind James is pointing out. List the corresponding James verses/passages.

Matthew / James	Connected Thought
a.	
b.	
c.	
d.	

5) What do you think James 4:5 means in relation to all of chapter 4?

Close out day one with reflection and prayer:

This is receiving the implanted Spirit.

"Or do you think that the Scripture says in vain, 'The Spirit who dwells in us yearns jealously?'" James 4:5 – In all we have read so far, this question from James is what it all comes down to: The more we understand it is God's love for us that compelled Him to send His Son and leave His Spirit, the greater our response is lived out in the same manner toward others.

Day Two

1) What kind of wisdom is being described in James 4:1-4?

2) What is the progression of living in the flesh?

3) Why is our friendship with the world considered spiritual adultery? (1 John 2:15-17; Hosea 1:1-3; 2 Corinthians 2:11:2; Jeremiah 13:27)

4. How do you think verse 5 fits with verses 1-4?

Close out day two with reflection and prayer. Share your thoughts:

"

For those who live according to the flesh set their minds on the things of the flesh, but those who live according to the Spirit, the things of the Spirit. For to be carnally minded is death, but to be spiritually minded is life and peace." Romans 8:5-6. Walking in the Spirit is to be in unity with the Spirit God planted in our hearts when we were born-again. When we are at war with the implanted Spirit, we will naturally be at war with one another. May this be on the rarest occasion.

Day Three

Pivot

Read James 4:5-10, then answer the following questions.

1) What is the message in these verses?

2) How does verse 5 relate to verses 6-10?

3) What do we learn about God's character and actions in these verses?

4) What step-by-step instructions are given in verses 7-10? Are they arbitrary or is there purpose in the order presented? Explain your answer.

James 4:6-9 is filled with Old Testament thought along with proverbs and psalms. His audience understood the depth of his words. As believers in Christ and recipients of grace, it was a call to remember grace is not to be taken negatively advantage of – as believers, they (we) should remember the grace of God cost Him the life of His Son – our Savior, Jesus Christ. James spoke to the outward (hands) and the inward (hearts and minds) in this section.

5) Read the following passages and note how they add insight to this section of scripture.

a. Psalm 138:6 & Proverbs 3:34:

b. Proverbs 6:16-19:

c. Exodus 19:10-11:

d. Exodus 30:17-21:

e. Leviticus 16:26-28:

"Purify your hearts, you double-minded… Vs 8c

a. 2 Corinthians 7:9-10:

b. Romans 8:

6) What beauty is found in the opening statement in verse 7 and the closing statement in verse 10?

7) Explain verse 5-10 in your own words.

Close out day three with reflection and prayer. Write out your thoughts:

"Or do you think that the scripture says in vain, the Spirit who dwells in us yearns jealously"? But He give more grace. Therefore He says: 'God resists the proud, but gives grace to the humble." James 4:5-6. Amen and amen. Lord, reveal the beauty of these truths to us in deeper ways that we would not resist and provoke your Spirit, but rather receive the working of the Spirit in greater ways as the deep things of God calls out to the deep parts of our soul (Psalm 42:7-8). This is how we pivot, dear sisters. From the flesh to the Spirit, living and growing as we are transformed into the image of Christ – a church ready for her groom.

Day Four

One Judge

1) What is the command in these verses?

2) To which "law" is James referring? (James 2)

3) How do you believe judging our brother is equal to speaking evil of, and judging the law?

4) Who is the Lawgiver and what "law" did he give?

5) How does judging our brother differ (or does it) from judging between right and wrong? Is James saying we are to excuse or condone sin?

Judging and making a judgment are often confused and abused in the church. We need to be mindful of the two types of judgment mentioned in scripture:

Judgment as being a judge of a person: Having the authority and knowledge to discern intent and understand the purpose/result of one's actions = Judgment to condemnation.

Making a sound judgment: Using godly wisdom to discern and respond to God's commandments and obey his word.

We are called to carefully, prayerfully, and graciously help our brothers and sisters who fall into sin. This is done for the purpose of restoration, not condemnation and is to be done out of love, while not approving of their sin—the way we hope others would do for us when we fall.

6) Read the following passages and note how they add to, or further define verses 11-12.

a. Matthew 7:1-5:

b. Romans 14:

c. Hebrews 10:30:

7) Read James 4:1-12, how do verses 11 and 12 fit with the previous topics? How might verse 7 & 10 help us to avoid judging our brothers and sisters in Christ?

Close out day four with reflection and prayer. Write out your thoughts:

Father, may we stand firm on the foundation of your love and live out your word with a humble and sincere heart so that we may be a fountain of fresh water to those around us. In the name of Jesus, amen.

Day Five

If the Lord Wills

1) What attitudes are contrasted in this section of scripture?

2) What is the relation to the previous statements in chapter 4?

3) Read James chapters 1-4:16. Do you see additional building of the underlying theme of this letter? What new insights have you gained up to this point? Share the passages that have taken on new understanding since you began this study.

4) Read verse 17. With the fresh reading of the book through 4:17, list the "good" that has been made known to you recorded in chapters 1-4. Note chapter and verse.

The "good"	The reference
a.	a.
b.	b.
c.	c.
d.	d.
e.	e.
f.	f.
g.	g.
h.	h.
i.	i.

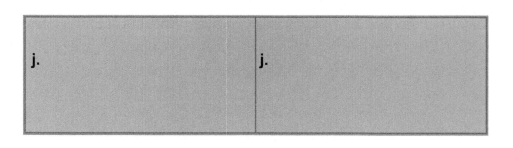

j.

j.

5) Read Psalm 39. How does this psalm reflect the attitude James described we should have toward the Lord?

6. Explain James 4:13-17 in your own words.

Close out day five with reflection and prayer. Write out your thoughts.

Day Six

A Jealous God Gives More Grace

"Or do you think that the scripture says in vain, 'The Spirit who dwells in us yearns jealously'? But He gives more grace. Therefore He says: God resists the proud but give grace to the humble. Therefore submit to God. Resist the devil and he will flee from you. Draw near to God and He will draw near to you." James 4:5-8a

These four verses sit between scolding and plea. James has been addressing doublemindedness and how living in the flesh (wisdom of men) and relying on their own strength was grieving the Spirit and causing the Spirit to yearn for them to return to Spirit-filled wisdom. The Spirit of God reflects His heart. James reminded them that God is a jealous God. It is not a human jealousy, but a pure jealousy driven by a deep concern for the welfare of His children and His Sovereign position. He was also reminding them that God is against pride and arrogance, and in essence sets His face against (resists) us when we are walking in our pride instead of humbleness. It was a call to submission and humility – a call to turn our face toward God, and in doing so, we are simultaneously turning our back (resisting) the devil. How is it possible to turn away from pride? By the "more grace" He gives. We can do everything He calls us to because no matter how great the fall, God's grace is bigger for those who humble themselves, submit, and draw near to God.

Read the following passages. Write out your thoughts on how they add to what James had to say about God's character and His faithful provision of grace.

1. Exodus 34:13
2. Deuteronomy 4:23-24
3. Psalm 78:58
4. Nahum 1:2
5. 2 Corinthians 11:2
6. Hebrews 4:16

7. 2 Corinthians 12:9
8. 2 Corinthians 9:8
9. John 1:16

Write out your thoughts:

Day Seven

Discuss this week's assignments and hold each other accountable in grace and prayer during this study (and always).

Discussion notes:

"Therefore be patient, my brethren, until the coming of the Lord. See how the farmer waits for the precious fruit of the earth, waiting patiently for it until it receives the early and latter rain. You also be patient. Establish your hearts, for the coming of the Lord is at hand." James 5:7-8

Week Six
The Implanted Patience

Day One

Patience Revisited

1) What topics does James mention?

2) How does the end of this letter relate to the beginning (chapter 1)? Note when James repeats similar thoughts or exact phrases (remember to include the reference). Do you think this repetition is significant?

3) To whom was James referring in verses 1-8?

4) What verse signals a shift in whom is being addressed throughout the rest of the chapter? Who is the message directed toward through the end of the chapter?

5) What new attributes of God are mentioned?

6) Read the entire book of James. How would you summarize the message and hope James gave to the early believers?

7) Keeping the themes of the book in mind, to what "healing" do you believe James was/is referring?

Close out day one with reflection and prayer. Share your thoughts:

Receiving the implanted patience.

Therefore be patient, my brethren, until the coming of the Lord. See how the farmer waits for the precious fruit of the earth, waiting patiently for it until it receives the early and latter rain. You also be patient. Establish your hearts, for the coming of the Lord is at hand." James 5:7-8 — Life has its struggles. Jesus promised as much. We live in a fallen world and we will suffer loss at the hands of others, as well as from our own sinful choices when we choose the flesh over the Spirit. The hope—the victory, however, is ours in Christ Jesus. He has a purpose for each of us and we are refined when we endure patiently. Just as James believed the coming of the Lord was at hand, so should we, remembering that He will give us the early and late rains (trials and blessings) that will cause us to reap a harvest. Wait on the Lord. Be of good courage, and He will bring it to pass.

Day Two

The Unrepentant Among the Brethren

Read James chapter 4:13 – 5:1-6, then answer the following questions.

1) What are the contrasting topics? How does James 4:16 connect the two?

2) How are arrogance and riches related? Is there a cause and effect? Explain your answer.

3) James spoke in the past tense when talking to the rich. What does it reveal about the condition of the heart of those people?

4) Read the following passages. Note how they add clarity to James 5:1-6.

a. Ezekiel 18:10-13:

b. Luke 6:24:

c. 1 Timothy 6:9:

4) What is the treasure the (wicked) rich pile up for themselves? (Romans 2:5)

5) What do you think did James meant when he said, "You have fattened your hearts"? Write out your current understanding before moving on to question 6.

6) Keeping with the understanding that James used a lot of Old Testament imagery, Proverbs, and Psalms, read the following passages and note how they add clarity and weight to James 5:5.

a. Deuteronomy 32:13-18:

b. Psalm 119:70:

c. Ezekiel 34:1-24:

Close out this day with reflection and prayer. Share your thoughts with the Lord:

Being rich is not a sin. It is the arrogant and greedy attitude that often sets in when the Lord is shunned, and self-righteousness sets in. James was calling the lost sheep to repentance (weep and mourn) and humble themselves before the Lord and receive His grace and deliverance from the road they were on. It serves as reminder to us to remain humble and love the Lord over any financial blessing that may come our way.

Day Three

Therefore Be Patient and Do Not Swear

Read James 5:7-12, then answer the following questions.

1) What topics did James mention?

2) What instructions did James give regarding their/our hearts?

3) Who are the ones that are blessed?

4) What is the difference between the heart of the arrogant and rich, and the heart of the brethren? (James 5:5 and James 5:8) How are each formed?

5) How many times did James reference the coming of the Lord? What do believe he was expecting? What does this say to us today?

6) James spoke of the Lord as Judge again in James 5:8. Read James 4:11-12. What was he reminding them of? How does James 5:8 add weight to James 4:11-12?

7) What attributes of God are mentioned in James 5:11? Why do you believe James stated these specific attributes at this particular point?

8) What is the final instruction in James 5:12? How does this fit with the topics James 5:1-12? How does this statement come full circle with the contrast of pride and arrogance focused on in chapter 4 through 5:12?

Close out this day with reflection and prayer. What has encouraged you and what has challenged you. Write out your thoughts:

Early rains – those that prepare the ground for growth, and the latter rains – those that cause maturity right before the harvest, speak to our lives. God calls us, establishes us, and then gives the increase – our perfected faith. May we be expectant of His return just as the early church was encouraged to do by Paul, Peter, James, and John. May we patiently endure, living out every moment for His glory and the blessing of others. May we be genuine followers and keepers of our word. In this, we will be living the royal law.

Day Four

We Must Pray

1) What is the topic of this section?

2) What specific instructions are given. List them in your own words.

3) How is prayer to be offered (or prayed)?

4) Look back at the entire message of James focusing on the contrasts we covered throughout this study. With the underlying theme in mind, to what kind/s of sickness and healing is James referring?

5) Read James 5:15-16. What is the progression of healing? What is the result?

6) How does James 5:13 sum up the entire message from James? Why do you suppose he made this statement at this point?

7) Read Isaiah 53:4-5: Make a list of what He took on (bore). Why was Jesus "pierced" or "wounded", "bruised" or "crushed"? What kind healing do His stripes provide? How does this add clarity to James 5:13-16?

8) James mentions prayer 7 times in the book of James – all 7 at the end of the book. Considering what believers have been called to do, why do you believe James closed out his message with the topic of prayer?

Close out this day with reflection and prayer. Write out your thoughts:

There is no question that Jesus heals physically. In context, however, it is important to remember that physical healing is not the promise of the cross. Spiritually healing is the promise. This is critical to understanding James 5:13-18 and the entire purpose of the message of endurance, faith, and the expectation of Christ's return as He works in our lives. In my opinion, James saved the high light of his message for the end. It is the perfect reminder that close fellowship with our Father through prayer, and our connection with our brothers and sisters in Christ through genuine service and honesty is what will give us the strength to endure life's hardships.

Day Five

The Look of Love

1) What topic is mention?

2) How does this topic differ from James chapter 4:11-12?

3) How is James 1:21-27 related to James 5:19-20?

4) How does James 5:19-20 fit with James 2:8?

5) How do these final instructions from James solidify the underlying themes of his message?

6) How are we "saving the soul" of another when we turn one away from the error of his way? How does this statement add understanding to what it is means to save the soul we have touched on throughout this study?

7) Read the following passages. How do they further explain the way we should help our brothers or sisters turn from the error of their ways?

a. Galatians 6:1:

b. Acts 20:28:

c. Matthew 18:15-17:

d. 2 Timothy 3:16-17:

8) What does this say to you if you are on the receiving end of correction? How should you respond?

Wrap it up

Go back to your commitments from the beginning of the study. Make a list of the way/s God responded to them.

1.

2.

3.

Write out a prayer of thanksgiving and a commitment of how you will use this new insight to serve others.

Day Six
A Deeper Look

By now we have read the book of James several times. We should be well acquainted with his message. With this, Lord willing, we were renewed in many ways as well as gained new perspectives and insights as the word of God is alive and active (Hebrews 4:12).

With this, read the book of James one final time (for this study). Note your closing thoughts on the book. What new insights did you gain? How has this book changed/increase your understanding of the message? After you write out your thoughts, compare them to week 1 and your initial read through notes and Matthew 5-7. Note specific differences, if any. Lastly, note how the Lord has used this to impact your behavior, or shine light on areas that need cleansing or healing. What will your nest steps be?

Close in prayer and write out your thoughts:

Day Seven

Discuss this week's assignments and hold each other accountable in grace and prayer during this study (and always).

Discussion notes:

Author's Closing Thoughts

Dear sisters in Christ,

It has been a joy praying for you as I was writing this study. I am humbled by all the Lord revealed to me through prayer and searching the scriptures each time I put pen to paper – so to speak. I was challenged in many areas as well as encouraged by the reminder of God's great love for me. My prayer throughout writing this study for you has been that you would be reminded of the same.

I recognize I have fallen short in conveying all this short but powerful book has to offer. Nevertheless, I pray God will grow you up and build upon the foundations we explored as you continue to surrender to His Lordship in your life.

Continue in His word. Study the book of James again and again and allow the Holy Spirit to reveal deeper understanding and fresh perspectives.

I am forever changed; I pray you are as well.

Until next time, may the Lord richly bless you in all spiritual understanding and give you wisdom as you live out your faith and may you allow His Spirit to water the Implanted Word until living out the royal law is what defines you – and me – and we are a bride prepared for her groom.

Feel free to write and share your thoughts with me. I welcome the feedback.

In Christ,

Teresa

Stonebridgepublications@outlook.com

Join us on Facebook for devotionals, studies, and prayer at The Implanted Word,
https://www.facebook.com/groups/76192357751729

Made in the USA
Middletown, DE
23 June 2021